THE GRENADA CAMPAIGN 1983 NAVY SEALS HOSTAGE RESCUE MISSION DURING THE GRENADA INVASION

Contents

Chapter 1 - Going to Medical School in the Caribbean

Going to the Medical School in Caribbean, Flashback 1982 – I arrived at Santo Domingo, DR. Went to hotel Naco. Met fellow Americans who told me about the Medical School Cetec and St George's Medical School in Grenada, which is an island not far from Dominican Republic and it is cheaper than Cetec University. I went to Cetec University Medical School in Arroyo Hondo. To see if I could get in. They told me I had to do two years of pre-medical school courses such as Sciences before I can be enrolled in the Medical School. So, I enrolled and went to the bulletin board where there were rooms for rent and a flyer of St George Medical School in Grenada with address and a message that it was cheaper than Cetec University for those students on a budget. I met a friend who told me about a room in a nice house very close by. I took the room. My friend told me the best way to get around is by motorcycle. So, I bought a motorcycle. Going to Medical school, I was supposed to be a man of learning – a scientist which brought up the topic of security and situational awareness. That meant I could not spend all my time at the clubs or pubs. There was in Marshall Arts School called Budo and Samurai and there was another school called Mi Yama Ryu Jujutsu. So, I enrolled in both of those for physical fitness. It turned out good for me.

Chapter 2 – A brief History of the land of Caribbean Pirates

Piracy in the Caribbean began in the 1500s. Piracy flourished in the Caribbean because of seaports like Port Royal Jamaica, Tortuga, St Lucia, Haiti, Nassau. 350 years ago, pirates like Drake, Henry Morgan, Black Beard in their quest for Gold and pieces of 8 of Spanish Main.

Chapter 3 - The beaches of the Dominican Republic

From Santo Domingo, I rode my bike to the beaches which is about an hour and forty-five minutes from the Capital. The beaches are Boca Chica, Gyacanas beaches. I thought of Cristopher Columbus landing here on the beach. Dominican Republic is rich in History. It was said that Henry Morgan had also landed here as well as many other pirates. The waters of the Caribbean are full of sharks and even more sharks of the coast of Jamaica. Every shark you can think of including a tiger shark as big as a school bus that can swallow a manhole. That is why the natives don't swim. Only the tourists. The natives say stay in the boat. I would get lost many times in santo domingo dr. how ever the natives were cool and the college age girls were even cooler. And would be glad to show a foreigner around, I met several nice girls and would go to clubs, bars, or just beers, . in santo domingo.dr. the area know as el malicone, by ocean is a place for festivals. Party night life. All night long. Dancing in the streets. Parades. Party town. Out side the capitol. There is purto plata. Another beach community.

Chapter 4 – Cetec University American Medical School of the Caribbean

Going to medical school in the Caribbean, there were lectures in the morning and in the afternoon were clinical rotations[lab] which were done in the hospitals with the supervision of a doctor in different specialties like Internal Medicine, Respiratory Medicine Ear Nose and Throat Medicine and Cardiology. Also, there was physical exam and medical diagnosis. All done in the hospital setting these clases done in the hospital know as clinical rotations were mandatory. As part of the course, thy in the Caribbean study the old fashion method. So for almost every class there was a clinical rotation. Hospital duty. It was very interesting, and learned a lot. There were other medical schools. Like cifas university in santo domingo, dr.

Chapter 5 – Caribbean Ocean blackholes rogue waves hurricanes Vortex

What is a worm hole ? craft disappearance into a worm hole in the Caribbean ocean unpredictable, at times huricanes, strong winds, electro magnetic storms, whirl pools giant, togue waves or monster waves at times

As far as the Caribbean Ocean hurricane winds, black holes, giant whirlpools, rogue waves are common unexpectedly. On Andros Island there is a navy base called Autec which is a navy base for testing and underwater research. Since 1960 alien connection. In 1950, an alien spaceship crashed very near what is now Autec navy base. It was reported that an alien survived but was covered up by the Bahamas Government because they felt it would scare the tourists. Since then, there have been many missing planes and many missing ships that have not been traced to date. There has been time warp. Missing time. So, the theory that an Alien operating like a pirate game has been in that sector for a long time. There is a story of a giant octopus. There is also a story of a shark octopus hybrid. Vodoo. Witchcraft is common on all the islands. Like the island of St Lucia and Cuba. In Cuba, there is a witchcraft where they worship a giant snake – an 80 ft Anaconda as part of the witchcraft religion. The snake protects a female who is in prison. Her name is Ochisi. Sometimes, as part of a sacrifice the witches let the snake swallow a manhole.

Chapter 6 – The Bermuda Triangle

What is a warm hole? Disappearing aircraft. In 1950, airlines lands with 92 skeletons on board. Flight 513, 1954, Santiago departs from Aachen West Germany destination to Purto Alegre, Brazil with a Government coverup. Book by Susan Reed entitled The body snatchers. Autec US Navy Base on Andros Island. The Atlantic undersea test and evaluation center Autec. Researchers believe that Autec is an underwater area 51. Some believe that there is an alien connection. Navy Squadron disappeared Flight 19 in the Bermuda Triangle. As for the alien, or reptilian still alive yes its possible. Could this alien reptilian, be running a gang in this sector . yes and for much of these island like st lucia, they believe in voodoo, witchcraft, thy worship the snake, and a reptilian, thy would embrac the alien and make him king of course, does the reptilian have powers yes he can fly, put people in a trance, loss of time, time warps, missing people, missing ships, missing planes, could the reptilian alien be doing this like the pirates of old yes, we have learned that all aliens are no tinthe same gang, thy have different agendas,

Chapter 7 – Seal team number 2 flying into ambush

President Reagan ordered troops to restore order on the island of Grenada where there was a coup and revolution led by the PRE Army led by General Hudson Austin. In a dictator quest for power. They had seven thousand troops armed with automatic rifles armed personal carriers and a tank of which they were scattered all over the island. In the process of hostile take over the people of Grenada had no guns. Therefore, they were sitting ducks. This revolution which was led by General Austin and Cuban Advisors as well as German Advisors as well as Russian Advisors were not taking any prisoners and were shooting people at random. There were dead bodies on every street. There were 1000 American Medical students on the island. They did not know that there was a Civil War. A revolution and a coup dta was going on. General Austin soldiers were rounding up the medical students to be used as bargaining chips or sold as sex slaves to Nigeria on the black market. They would fetch a very good price. Seal team 6 is going to lead the way. The Seals Team number 1 mission to plant Beacons to illuminate the runway for transport C130S AND Choppers. They are to parachute in the ocean. Very similar to what the path finders did in World War II. They did however Hurricane winds monster waves whirlpools as the Seals loaded with equipment fought to free themselves from the parachute before being drowned in the ocean and taken to the bottom of the ocean before they would get dragged under. Four seals died. It is believed they drowned or eaten by the sharks in the water.

Chapter 8 - 1983 a coup was forming in the Island of Grenada

Maurice Bishop, a leader of the Country of Grenada and his cabinet were arrested and later executed by General Hudson Austin. In 1983, rebel soldiers -the PRE Army took over the Island under General Austin, a dictators quest for power. Grenada is a British Commonwealth. Governor Scoon is the UK Representative. The PRE Army was watching Governor Scoon's residence. They had check points for the forty infantry soldiers with automatic weapons and armored personal carrier. Seal team number 2 under command Commander Dillon flying into an ambush landed. They fast roped on Governor Scoon's mansion. As they landed in front of the house, the shoot out began. They went inside Governor Scoon's house as they began to fight their way home. The Seals landed with just 5 minutes to spare. As the shootout went on, some Seals were wounded. The Seals were themselves shooting about 19 PRE-Soldiers as they were mad. The Seals fought back to hold off these Pirates from taking over. The Seals used the phone to call the States for evacuation of Governor Scoon. Governor Scoon was successfully evacuated by Seal team 6 - Number 2 Seal Team.

Chapter 9 – Seal team 6. Team number 3

Seal Team 6. Number 3 Team and Sergeant Highway's marine security detachment were ordered to rescue 19 Medical students still somewhere on the island. Little is known of this mission since many of the things that Navy Seals do is secret. This is their story.

The Seals swim in as the battleship is peppering the island with artillery fire. As the Seals begin to swim to the war zone, the Marine security detachment job was to make sure and clear the way for the seals to get close to the hostages. As the Seals were experts in HRT(Hostage Rescue Techniques), I was on the other side of the island at a check point because the PRE-Army had roadblocks and were telling the people to surrender. I figured I am an American. They can deport me. As I saw many people in front of me surrender at gun point. As I looked around, I saw dead bodies on every street. It was creepy. We didn't have a choice. I heard shooting, yelling as I advanced with my hands up, they shot the people in front of me. Then I was in shock realizing that they were not taking prisoners. As a hail of bullets hit the wall next to me. As I looked at the tank, I could see the machine gun beginning to move towards me and the soldiers pointing at me. So, I ran into the neighborhood down the street hoping that this army would lose interest in me. No way. These were a hunter force of the army in a hostile takeover. As I ran down streets trying to lose these guys zigzagging all the way. By afternoon, I was tired. I could see soldiers still pointing at me and waiting for the tank to follow. I was worried. So, I ran by the beach. While running by the beach, I saw another dead body. So, I kicked him. He said – "Ouch!" And I looked down at him and I said, "You are alive?" He said" Yes! I am a marine". And I said "What the Heck buddy! We are going to get killed in three minutes. There was a patrol and a tank right behind me. He said "Don't worry. The Nave Seals are here. "I looked around and I didn't see nobody. Nothing but the ocean. "Are you sure?" He hands me a shiny 45 Gun. "Here! Defend yourself." For me, that was a turning point. Now there is hope. He said "Quick! Into the ocean." We jumped under water into the ocean. I, knowing that the ocean is full of sharks. We were under water few minutes and the patrol went right past us. Sergeant Highway said "Quick! To the church. We will hold up there" He said, "They are after you bad!" Sergeant Highway said "You can go down to the beach and watch the seals swim in." So, I did. As the Seals assembled on the beach. They surrounded me and asked me to join them. "Help us find the hostages". As artillery fire rocked the island I said, I would. There is a bond between soldiers on a battlefield. Knowing that somehow, we will get through this. There was a dispute between the marines and the Navy Seals. Sergeant Highway said it's the seal's mission. So, they will leave the way. "Ed, take one of the Seals and find those hostages." The Seals knew about me, and they said "Hey Man! They set you up as a fall guy. I said "Wow! You guys have information that I don't have." So, me and the seal went for a hike. After a while, the Seals stops. He nods with his head. Working with Seals – I noticed that they are men of few words. They work by Telepathy and a single nod. I was "What does that mean? You want me to go over there? The Seal is looking up at the ceiling now and mumbling a few words to himself. Then he runs to the school locker room where there are two guards with rifles and the Seal breaks his neck. As the other guard runs inside yelling "There is a guy out here who killed a man." And the Seal said "Why didn't you shoot?" I said " I was over a 150 feet away. Too far." Again, the Seal is looking at the ceiling again. He says" This guy coming out is yours. You do one and I do one all the way back. I am not getting killed on this island because of you." I said "Okay" as I entered the university locker room. It was dark I saw a girl she was looking at me up and down. I said to her is there any more of you she said yes, there is 19 of us, I said were, she said over here, as I walked into the locker room to my amazement there were 19 girls medical school students sitting down very quite. I would never have found them thy were so quite. So I made a speech, girls we have to go to the boat, because there is a war going on. It is quite dangerous right now for americans, many people have been killed. And the navy has a dinner for you and party the navy seals will take you there. The girls cheered, lets go girls. And there was a man in the corner of the room. He said im not going, and can I see your gun I said no, and that your right, but your in a combat zone, good luck again he said there is a name on that gun.. I said its mine. No slip ups im working for the seals this time, lets go. And I threw a rifle to that man. I did not recognize him today I know who that man was it was drew gomer . cow boy from new Mexico.. the girls said are you a pirate I said no im with the navy, as we went to the boat. Hey sgt. Highway look what we got. All the sailors jaw drooped. There girls. Yes isaid. Sgt highway said quick get in the raft. Sailors swim. As we said good by I could see the seals felt sorry for me. Because I stayed on the island.

In Conclusion, Seal Team 6 the number 3 Team and Seargent Highways marine detachment their mission was successful. And I believe one of the Medical Students upon landing on the US Airport kissed the ground. Prime Minister Margaret Thatcher of England criticized President Reagan for acting too hastily. It was a good thing that President Regan acted the way he did because the Seals had only minutes to rescue people's lives. If he had waited, there would be many more people killed. President Regan thought it was a threat to national security. On February of 2020, I, Edward Vargas, sent an email to the

White House requesting President Biden that he award Seal Team 6 and myself and Sergeant Highways marine detachment be awarded the Medal of Honor.

The Author writing his story

The Map of the War Zone

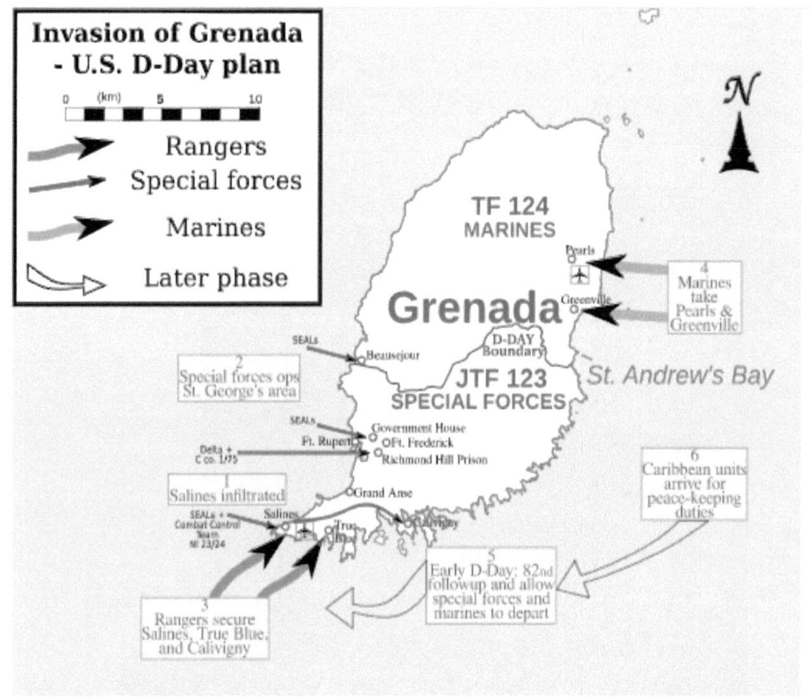

Navy SEALs in Grenada Operation URGENT FURY

Black seal on white sand

Medical Students of Grenada

A student from the Saint George's University School of Medicine in Grenada is

A student from the Saint George's University School of Medicine in Grenada

A student from the Saint George's University School of Medicine in Grenada

A student from the Saint George's University School of Medicine in Grenada

Students from the Saint George's University of Medicine in Grenada are

A group of well-wishers wait on the flight line to greet students from the Saint

A group of well-wishers wait on the flight line to greet students from the Saint

A group of well-wishers wait on the flight line to greet students from the Saint

Students from the Saint George's University of Medicine in Grenada are

Students from the Saint George's University School of Medicine in Grenada conduct

A group of well-wishers wait on the flight line to greet students from the Saint

A group of well-wishers wait on the flight line to greet students from the Saint

The U.S. Invasion of Grenada: Legacy of ...
facebook.com

Watch Navy Seals: The Untold Stories ...

U.S. Marines in Grenada 1983 PCN ...

Grenada | Operation urgent Fury ...

OPERATION
GRENADA
1983
URGENT FURY

U.S. NAVY SEALS
The Untold Stories
GRENADA

The Telegraph

Governmental & Military

AUTEC

means

Atlantic Undersea Test & Evaluation Center

by acronymsandslang.com

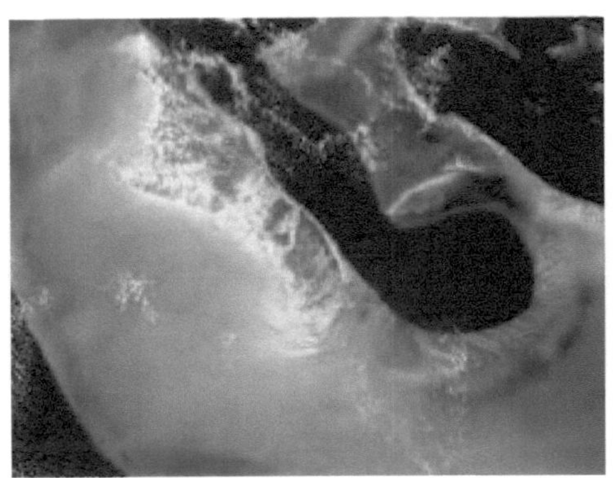

Atlantic UFO Incident ...

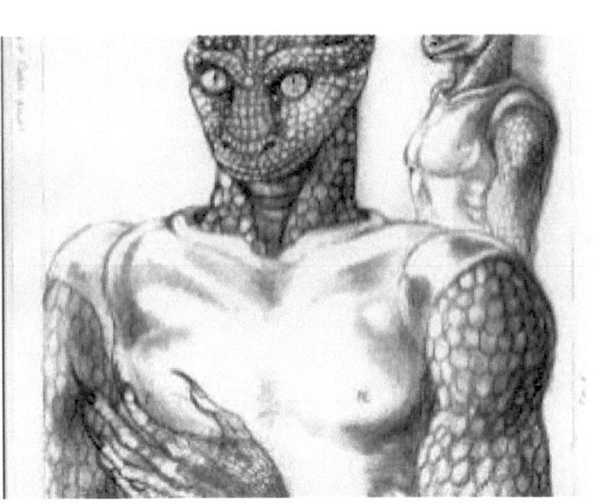

www.ingramcontent.com/pod-product-compliance
Ingram Content Group UK Ltd.
Pitfield, Milton Keynes, MK11 3LW, UK
UKHW042002190726
13854UKWH00005B/2123

9 798416 479091